VIRTUAL MEETINGS

**Set them up. Lead them well.
Reach your goals.**

VIRTUAL MEETINGS

Set them up. Lead them well.
Reach your goals.

Antoni Lacinai
Mike Darmell

Table of contents

○ "Virtual meetings...
so what?"

Ericsson asked...
Telia asked...
Volvo asked

> "We know you can help us get better
> at leading meetings. But what advice
> can you give on virtual communication?
> Virtual leadership? Virtual meetings?"

We squirmed a bit and gave a few quick tips, explaining that 80% are the same. But the other 20%... well, we didn't really have much to say about that. Because the truth is that we are not too fond of virtual meetings!

Maybe we shouldn't say that – especially to you, who just bought this book. Not to you, who might well think virtual meetings are the best invention since sliced bread.

We have a preference for physical (meatspace) meetings and believe in their power to drive people and organisations forward, but we realise they aren't always practical, economical or good for the environment; road, rail or air, you spend time and money, and leave a carbon footprint. Of course, many of us would like to scrap meetings altogether, but it's undeniable: interaction with colleagues (clients, suppliers, 'partners' in general) is important – wherever they are. Virtual meetings are an opportunity to communicate, discuss, strategise and build rapport – whatever the distances, however scattered the participants. Companies and organisations with 'global reach' spread across multiple locations and time zones use virtual meetings, remote teamwork, cloud-based collaboration spaces… all challenges to people – like you, probably – who place a high value on good communication between individuals, across silos and within groups.

With so many of our clients asking the same question, we accepted that it is time to delve deep into virtual meetings. We have interviewed wise, knowledgeable, experienced people; we've read their books and others', and trawled the Internet; we've asked ourselves and drawn on our own experience –as employees of big companies and as independent consultants. As consultants, we've asked our clients what success factors and pitfalls they see.

And now, we have developed this guide for you who lead or participate in virtual meetings.

Note: This is not a technical manual for Adobe, Cisco, Microsoft, Citrix, telephone switches or any other product/technology. Not at all. Technology develops and changes constantly. The book would be old before it was printed (or downloaded).

Instead, it is a three-part manual:
1. Useful advice regardless of the type of meeting
2. Practical tips regardless of virtual technology
3. Concrete tips (and warnings) for each technical solution – tool, app, online forum

You use this book as a starting point – a source of knowledge and a trigger for ideas. Pick and choose, don't just try and follow these procedures blindly. As the Albanian saying goes:

> *Take advice from 200 men,*
> *then do what you yourself think is best!*

Maybe this will come as a disappointment. One CEO asked if we could provide a complete rulebook for his 30,000 employees. We said No. (Dear CEO, If you like you can buy this book for your employees and have a number of workshops where you derive your own optimal policy – a How-To, within which your people will take pride in ownership. Try it. Rejoice in your better-performing, dedicated staff. Measure the profit from the efficient, productive meetings and rejoice again!).

Out of all the tips that follow, choose those that suit you best. Meanwhile, if you come up with any approaches that you want to use that are not in this book, use them too. And feed them back to us, if you have a moment.
Email:
antoni@lacinai.se
micke.darmell@gr8meetings.se

Who are the we?

Antoni Lacinai is the communications expert who is helping good people and organisations achieve their goals by improving their engagements with others. Typical topics for his lectures, seminars and coaching include presentation technique, successful customer calls, the art of performing better by setting the right goals and the craft of leading team meetings. He moderates conferences and workshops and writes books, blogs and chronicles about communication and motivation.

Mike Darmell is the meeting evangelist with over 20 years' experience in the meetings industry. Starting off as a nurse, Mike changed career to marketing and event management. For seven years he has been running the company gr8 meetings, helping organisations to boost internal meetings – efficiency and effectiveness. He is also one of the most sought-after lecturers in how non-stop connection affects us.

Together we also authored the book *"Make Meetings Work"* (2015), which you can find on Amazon.

> *Our purpose:*
> *to help you have better meetings at work*

Our goal with this guide is to give you tools, insights and tips that help you bring more energy, efficiency and creativity to your virtual meetings.

What do we mean by…?

Video meetings
Where you each have a camera and you can all see each other. Everyone can join the conversation.

Phone meetings
Where you only hear each other. These days, it's often Skype without webcam. Everyone can be in on the call.

Webcast
For example, YouTube or Bambuser. Some are gathered together, some are scattered. Not everyone can participate on the same terms.

Webinar
Like a virtual cinema… a seminar delivered over the Internet. One is talking, the rest – scattered – can watch (or at least listen). The chat function can be used, as well as video – up to a point.

Shared desktop
Where everyone in the virtual meeting can share PowerPoint slides, virtual whiteboard, etc.

Synchronous communication
Online here-and-now communication. A 'live' meeting.

Asynchronous communication

Online>offline>online – for example, e-mail or voicemail. (Back in time: letter, telegram or fax.)

What are the experts' views?

Not too clear, actually. Indistinct, fuzzy, ambiguous, slanted.

Experts in virtual communication think (not so surprisingly) that virtual meetings rock! To that extent, they agree. Some even say that virtual meetings are not just as good as but much better than physical meetings.
But after that it starts getting less clear-cut – notably regarding which medium is best. Phone? Phone-plus-internet? Video? Web and chat? Some say that phone meetings lack the body-language benefit; you can't see the other people's gestures and facial expressions. Quite so, say others – and that's a good thing because a video link carries a lot of distracting stuff like gestures and facial expressions (so if you're on Skype, kill the camera!).

Many think that good old-fashioned face-to-face physical meetings are needed but not every time. A bit of both, virtual and real, as and when required. There's no denying the gains to be had from a proper get-together, properly conducted: shake hands or hug, feel the mood, transmit eyeball-to-eyeball honesty, share coffee & cake, beer & pizza, exotic local specialities. (The cost of such trifles is touched on below.)

Pros and cons
of virtual meetings

There are upsides and down. For sure, some meetings (IT in Beijing + HR in Bangalore + BD in Bogota + …) might never take place without all this amazing technology. Time for a list:

Pros:

+ **It's better for the environment** because we save energy, produce less CO_2/SO_2, burn fewer worn-out tyres.
+ **We save time.** Imagine travelling for a couple of hours or even days to participate in a 30-minute meeting.
+ **We save money** on air fares, taxis, hotels, rounds of drinks…
+ **We become more productive.** That travelling time – even with a laptop or tablet on the go – is surely less fruitful than staying where you really belong and doing what you're best at.
+ **The right people can participate.** The brightest and best in the organisation are usually in demand; they don't find it easy to leave base for a couple of days to join a buzz-group 1000 miles away. But to close the office door for an hour and log on to the real-time meeting you have organised? No problem!
+ **We can act quicker.** If there is an emergency we can't always wait for all the people to travel all the way to HQ/command centre/conference plaza.

+ **We can avoid long-drawn-out gatherings.** The technology allows more frequent, shorter and sharper sessions... and maybe even sweeter? This book has a few recipes – all low-carb.

Cons:

– **Poor communication.** Especially the unspoken stuff: emotions glad or sad, nods of approval or pained winces, the steady gaze that disappears when people are looking at the monitor instead of the camera... And is that woman in Birmingham checking her smartphone under the desk instead of looking at the finance director's slides?

– **Participation and contribution are stifled.** The participants find it just a bit harder to chip in, and the chair/moderator/facilitator finds it just a bit harder to draw them in. Charisma, empathy, sensitivity... no icon to tap on!

– **Technical hiccups.** Interruption, distraction, frustration, impatience.

– **The social, touchy-feely thing evaporates.** No campfire, no pool table, no espresso machine.

– **It does cost money.** Cheaper than personal travel, sure. But numbers of scattered people paying for upgrades and maybe the hire of a webinar conference room? Well, it isn't entirely free.

– **It's harder to stay focused.** With emails dropping in or a colleague popping his head round the door (or even the dog barking, if you're working at home today), can you really keep up with the dialogue between your colleagues in Manchester and Moscow?

– **It's boring.** We'll be showing you that it doesn't have to be horribly tedious, but all too often there's one participant droning on and another dozing off. Certainly, a lot of people sign in with low expectations, and their gloom and despondency can be infectious.

– **If you're not good at it it's going to fail.** Inexperienced, under-skilled leaders and untrained, incompetent participants can wreck a virtual meeting more easily than a real physical one.

"What you win in social power, you lose in time"
Bengt Littorin, Swedish Environmental Protection Agency

When to meet virtually and when to meet physically

Do a cost-benefit analysis – with quality of communication a major factor. Communicate virtually when you want to save money, travel time, the planet.

Communicate across or around a real table when all the important people can get there and/or there are complex issues to thrash out and/or the budget isn't too tight.

1.
General advice
on meetings

General advice on meetings

A meeting is a meeting, right?

Our experience tells us that 80-20 rule applies when we compare real and virtual meetings; most of what goes well or goes wrong is true in both environments. So we'll start by giving you advice that applies in either.

But wasn't this to be a book about virtual meetings?

Our point is that good meetings are based on good preparation. Many of our top tips apply regardless of the type of meeting. It's possibly even more important to prepare for a virtual meeting than for a physical one. Therefore, we can't skip the basics. We'll start there and then we will focus on the tips and techniques specific for virtual meetings.

Make time for planning

20 years ago we could say that we would plan the meeting on Thursday – and then we did it on Thursday. Today the job list and calendar are under much greater stress; the urgent-important prioritisation wobbles hour by hour, minute by minute. Emails were the turning point, and since then, with all that pressure, how can you keep the Plan the Meeting slot safe?

Plan time to plan

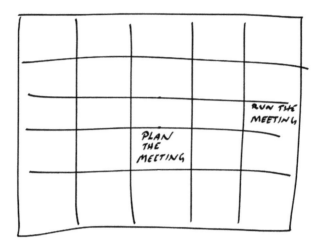

PLAN
THE
MEETING

RUN THE
MEETING

The same way you book a time for a meeting you should book some time for planning. Write it down in your calendar/diary – on the wall, in your pocket diary or app. Hovw much time? There is no telling; it depends on what you have in mind for the meeting and who is participating. The more complicated the meeting, the more information and opinion the people will bring, the more crucial the outcome, the more time you need to plan. Quite likely you will need longer to plan a meeting than to hold the meeting.

Of course some meetings are routine. There may be a quick Hello, a quick and painless exchange of information, and a Thank-you. You should still plan. Do you have the right conditions – technology and timing? The right people? Proper procedures? The right purpose and goals? That last thing is what we'll get into now.

Decide the purpose and the goal of the meeting

What is the purpose of the meeting? What's it for? What's it all about? Where will it lead? Even when it seems obvious (obvious to you yourself, that is!) it's well worth spending time formulating it – making it clear and specific in your own overworked, multi-tasking mind. Only then can you get the message to every participant. This is our top tip – the key to better meetings! Today about 44% of our meetings lack clear purpose and objectives (says the Meeting Quality Index).

Purpose

You should start by understanding:

> *Why are we having this meeting at all?*

The purpose. You must be able to answer the question *Why?* It's not wrong to answer more than once – getting a grip on the thing.

The reason for the meeting? If your own answer is *To inform,* then ask: Why should I inform? And why these people? And what will they do with the information? And what will go wrong if they don't have the information? And why not just send them the information in an email? *To inform* is not a reason or a purpose in itself. Dig deeper.

A real purpose with a real meaning will give both you and the participants positive energy, because we'd rather do things that are meaningful. Meaningless? Oh, one of *those* meetings…

Once you have figured out the real underlying reason, you might have realised (to pursue the same example) that the purpose was *not* to inform but, perhaps, to work together towards beating all the other companies on customer satisfaction. That purpose would have an effect on the content of the meeting. In the real world, to sit passively at a briefing meeting and absorb the stuff is boring and demotivating. In a virtual set-up, it's much worse.

Rethink it! Maybe you should send out the dry information in advance – simple, clear, well edited – and spend the meeting time on sharing reactions, pooling ideas, making decisions, agreeing action plans...

Goal

What are you trying to achieve?

The goal. The gurus in goal-psychology Locke & Latham found that people's performance improves by 15-30% if the right goals have been set, and instilled in the individual and his co-workers.

Just imagine the difference for the participants in a meeting if they know what they are trying to achieve. A goal should be firm, within your control, easy to measure, preferably attractive and challenging. That brings focus, commitment and higher productivity. A goal model you can use to make your group perform at its best is HAPPY:

H = Hard. Yes, really. Hard but not impossible. If it's too easy, you don't need to work for it. If it's too hard, you won't even try. Of course when you start off your journey, you can break it down into step-by-step sub-goals. That builds momentum.

A = Attractive. You either want to run away from something bad or you want to move toward something good. From a motivation and energy perspective, it is almost always better – more fun – to strive towards something great.

P = Precise. Synonyms: Clear, Specific, Measurable. This is the crucial factor. The other bits in this Five-Letter Acronym are performance enhancers, but without the goal being precise, it is just a strategy, a philosophy or a vision... a bit of wishful thinking.

P = Punctual. A goal without a deadline is more often than not a dream. Better to have an agreed timeframe and an end-date – project management overlap, here… Gantt chart and progress checks.

Y = Yours. A goal within your control is often more motivating than if it is outside in the hands of others, the market, the world economy, them up-stairs. If the "what" goal is a biggy, and you don't hold all the cards, turn it somehow into one or more "how" goals – things you *do* have control over, and where you *can* make things happen… things that make a difference in the big picture. This makes a huge difference to the mood of the meeting; when you say *you* or *we* it's a call to action.

If this is too complicated, then at least ask yourself the question: *What needs to happen once the meeting is finished?*

Plan your milestones
Once you have reflected and decide on the big WHYs, you take the next planning steps – putting on your project manager hat.
- When will you send invitations? What will they contain? *
- When will you send preparatory information and material? *
- When will you send the gentle reminder?
- When will you book the IT support, if you need it? If not,
- When will you be on-site, with all the technology set up and tested?
- Will you appoint a note-taker?
- When will you do the tidy-up, the distribution of notes, and the progress chasing?
- When will you reflect on the other things – facts and feelings?
- When will you invite feedback – opportunities for improvement, espe-cially?

*How long in advance do you need to send out the invitations, information and other materials? It varies, of course. If you have regular meetings with the same participants, ask them. Some want an invitation three days before, others maybe three weeks. Respect those needs; these are all busy people juggling their calendars!

And hey, remember to communicate the meeting's purpose and goals in your invitation!

Prepare the right methods... to suit the meeting

We believe in the power of involvement. To create participation. It gives energy. We also believe in a clear process, and good meeting leaders who can control the meeting in both preparation and execution. You, dear reader. To set up effective procedures you should be clear about:

1. The purpose of the meeting
2. The objective of the meeting
3. Who you invited and who is coming
4. Of them, who knows what, and how much they know about each other
5. How much time you – and they – can spend in the meeting
6. The virtual venue – technical conditions, confidentiality, possible interruptions

If you have free rein, maybe you can choose methods based on 1-4 and then decide 5 and 6 yourself – although you will often have to modify your wishes given limited resources.

Involvement gives energy

If you only intend to deal out or share information (not an ideal goal, as such meetings tend to be boring and participants only half-remember what has been said), the trick is to choose a simple, clear medium. Most people use PowerPoint for this.

It's a different thing when discussion, reflection and decision-making are on the agenda. Monologue plus PowerPoint overload – from you or any one of the others – will kill the meeting. The well-informed, creative team member with the key to the problem might not get a word in before close-down. Chairmanship, moderation, facilitation, mediation, note-taking – they all require planning.

Choose methods that meet your needs, and impose them with a light touch. Gently nudge, don't push or kick.

Examples of methods:

- Presentations
- Speaking one at a time
- Beehives
- Brief contributions in the chat window, then a group discussion
- Voting
- Creative exercises to come up with fresh ideas for a familiar challenge
- Energisers to lighten the mood
- An ice breaker at the start so they all know this is to be an open, enjoyable, useful session

Be on time

When we lecture we often ask the audience to come up with their (least) favourite ways to ruin a meeting. Late arrival is always in the top (bottom?) three – along with phone/tablet distractions and irrelevant jibber-jabber.

Be there on time; be done in time.

In time means you should be *done* with all the preparations five minutes before the meeting starts. Before kickoff you should check:

- Are the computers, phones, connections etc working?
- Do I really know – and understand – the agenda?
- How will I start the meeting?
- When will I bring up the reasons and the goals for the meeting?
- When do I explain the rules we'll be playing by?
- Should I play some music before the meeting starts to create a more relaxed atmosphere?

We realise that many rely on Outlook, where each meeting begins and ends dead on the hour. If you have a meeting that ends just as another starts you (and they) have no time to get ready. It's very hard to be in two places at once – physically or virtually. Aim to complete a 'one-hour' meeting in

40-45 mins. (They won't complain. It's your job as meeting leader to create the right conditions, so the goals can be reached *in time,* not *bang on time.*)

If you do that, you will avoid a lot of stress. This is especially true of virtual meetings, where technical hiccups are all-too-likely. More about that later…

See and smile

Humans are herd animals. We want to feel we are recognised – seen as part of the whole. Our cousins, the apes, work about four hours a day to gather food. When they reconvene, they look each other in the eye or else things get tense in the group. For all that we humans are well-practised in containing – or concealing – our emotions, the bottom line is the same: we want to be seen and welcomed.

> *Welcome the participants*

Our common friend Jan Gunnarsson does nothing but talk about the concept of 'hostmanship' in his lectures and books. There are good reasons for that; people who feel welcome will be more positive and open to new ideas; people who are in a good mood perform better, boosting productivity, profitability, or any other of the organisation's key performance indicators. It is simply profitable to have a welcoming, hospitable culture.

If you have finished your preparations in good time, so you are comfortable and confident, you can focus on the participants rather than technical problems. *See and smile* is a good expression. Purely in a literal sense, it is easy to project or observe a smile in the physical or video meeting, but even on the phone, we think you can see and smile. You can hear if a person is feeling good or grumpy. If you as the meeting leader are in a good mood, that will infect the participants.

Agree on your meeting rules
- Is it okay to read mail during a meeting?
- Is it okay to be late for a meeting?
- Is it okay for the leader to stop conversations that aren't leading anywhere?
- Is it okay to show emotions or is it to be a flat, dead focus on the matter at hand?
- Is it okay to leave the meeting for a while, rejoining later?
- Is it okay not to have a goal for every meeting?
- Is it okay to abort a meeting?
- Is it okay to speak in a phone meeting without saying your name?
- Is it okay to express complaints without offering a solution?
- Is it okay to try to address one item meeting after meeting?
- Is it okay always to have the meeting when it suits the leader, even if some participants are in time zones that mean late night/early morning sign-in?
- Is it okay to run over the planned time if you don't get everything sorted?
- Is it okay to break (or bend) the meeting rules? What happens if you do?

Agree and act thereafter

We may have our own answers to the questions above – the way we play the game in our own business affairs – but they will not be strictly relevant to you in yours. What is relevant is what you decide to apply to your department, your meetings, your organisation – the 'ways of working' you have agreed on. Praise each other for sticking to those rules, and ensure there are consequences for those who don't. An organisation one of us was worked with once introduced a special "punishment" for those who were late: the rest of the group chose a song-and-dance routine and the person who was late had to perform it at the end of the meeting. Since those who worked there were no showman-artists, people started to be on time. We're not advocating a similar form of 'retributive justice', but surely there should be a gentle rap on the knuckles for those who don't play the game. Find your own way to make your agreement work!

In longer meetings: have some breaks and energisers in the plan

All monotonous communication numbs us. Our brains go to sleep mode, and our focus wanders – more quickly now than in earlier generations. The attention span is only a few minutes.

Even if you are a skilled meeting leader with many different methods at your disposal, participants will sometimes lose energy – especially as that long meeting drags on. Remember to build pauses into the agenda.

Decent breaks are more important for physical meetings than virtual ones, because they bring an excellent opportunity to build relationships. But even in a virtual meeting, as the digital clock in the corner of the screen moves on, it is important to have a breather on the balcony, a toilet break, a coffee top-up, a smoke... We are not robots, and if our basic needs are not satisfied (coffee counting as a basic need for many of us), our cravings will swamp our awareness, drowning the dutiful drive to follow the meeting. Five minutes every now and then, please.

For longer physical meetings it may also be good to have two different kinds of breaks:
- 'Relationship break' where you have time to socialise with others and take refreshment together.
- 'Job-break' where you are can check your email, send a text message or make that vital phone call.

To go back to the Energiser idea... Many tools for virtual meetings provide quiz features and buttons for voting. Throw in a fun quiz about the topic under discussion, or ask for immediate feedback on a topic by voting. Interactivity makes it more fun and keeps participants alert. Here's some more about that!

Create participation and interaction

There is a simple model for leadership that one of the writers got from a leadership programme a couple of years back. This is what it looks like:

$$ I \rightarrow I \rightarrow I $$

Involve → Inform → Implement

Simplicity... genius!

- If you **Involve a lot**, you don't need to **Inform a lot** (since everyone was involved in the process), so the group is ready, willing and able to **Implement** the *group's* mutual decision.
- If you don't **Involve a lot**, you need to **Inform a lot** (top-down monologue) which leaves the group feeling hesitant, even reluctant, to **Implement** your decision.

This does not mean that every goal to be set, every decision to be made, should permeate through every layer and section of the organisation. Some goals come from above and are set. These are often called outcome goals or *What*-goals (increased sales, bigger market share, percentage increase in efficiency, *etc.*). What you can do in such cases is create involvement by allowing the group to set their *How*-goals, *i.e.* the things that can be done to optimise everyone's chances of achieving the What-goals.

Are you a leader of meetings? Find methods that convert what your What-goals to How-goals. Use meeting time for this. It's time well invested.

Give information asynchronously. Treat information synchronously.

Good meetings are both effective and give more energy than they take. 'Synergy', they call it. Pure briefings packed with boring, obscure PowerPoint slides are neither effective nor inspiring. (We've all suffered some of that.)

Use the precious meeting time to discuss, reflect and decide. But to get them there, some form of information is needed.

Give out information in advance

Mail the material to everyone who might need it, whether it's a PowerPoint deck, a Word document, a well-structured email, a link to a specific page on a website or a YouTube video. Ask them to get in the starting-blocks for the meeting by investing a few minutes in advance.

The argument against this is that they – or some of them – won't read it or view it.

If you see it that way it's time to ask yourself: *Why?* Dig until you know the reason (not the excuse). Ask yourself: Do we have too many informative meetings? *How do I want it instead?* Redo it and do it right. Build it into your 'ways of working' and let them all know that there will be consequences (*see above*) if they turn up for the meeting without having done their preparatory homework.

Finish on time

Do you often think *"there's a lot I need to do right now... lots on my plate"*?

Newsflash: there won't be any less. Everybody has a lot to do. We are always working towards something. To go beyond the decided finish time isn't a great strategy. It just shows you can't keep a meeting together within the agreed limits and with the desired quality.

On the other hand, if you make a safe and smooth landing five minutes before the time is up, it shows that you are a good meeting leader – respectful of other people's priorities and all the stuff they have on their plates.

Sometimes, time can fly away even for the most experienced meeting leader. A subject that takes much longer than you anticipated, crucial and urgent matters arising. When this happens you have to make a choice: postpone some of the agenda items, or cut in and stop the 'digression'. Maybe by now you have a meeting rule that allows you to take some more time. That's up to you. Or here's another tip: don't plan your agenda down to every last second:

Create an agenda filled to 80%

Then the problem will only occur rarely, and if you should finish a bit ahead of time, everyone will be happy.

Summarize and reflect

Use the last five-ten minutes to summarize the meeting and reflect over what went well procedurally and what might be improved. Accentuate the positive; use most of those minutes on what went well. What we are happy about, we want more of, and that creates a positive feedback culture.

Do what you agreed to do

If the meeting is supposed to bring you closer to your goals and be useful for the organisation, the customers, the citizens, the farmers, the pupils or whoever, it's not enough to just have a meeting. You need to actually do what has been agreed.

If you are having meetings that aren't leading anywhere, you might as well call it coffee time.

Before anyone leaves the meeting you need to be clear about who is going to do what and when it needs to be done.

If there is free space in your calendar, or pre-planned time for your Action Points (tasks/missions/follow-ups) it's easier. If not, it's about time you got a grip on your time-planning.

2.
General Advice
Regardless of
Virtual Technology

General advice regardless of virtual technology

Picking up on our line earlier – that 80% of all good meetings are good in the same ways, in planning and execution – that leaves 20% of factors differentiating the virtual meeting from the physical.

Before we put forward concrete communication tips (and self-exploratory questions) for this or that modern/high-tech channel, here are some that apply across the board: video-conference or telephone conference.

Send a gentle reminder

The experts agree that it's good to remind the people just one extra time if it's a virtual meeting. After all, they're not going to see you across the office or in the elevator as a memory-jogger.

Remind yourself to remind them

So it's good to put a note in your own calendar, to send out a reminder just before the meeting. Those who forgot or overlooked emails now have another chance to join the meeting.

If there was documentation, or a link, in your first mail you should include that in the reminder, to save them the trouble of trawling their system to find it.

We have already discussed this and – be honest now – how often have you failed to read through the material before the meeting? Don't be falsely optimistic; your participants are built the same as you. This is not us being mean; we're all suffering information overload and we're all prone to sins of omission.

This problem goes on until you have restructured your meeting culture. A reminder including possible material helps the participants to do it better, preparing for your meeting.

Cultivate the relation and not just the question at hand

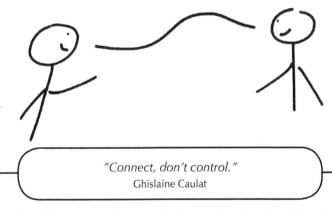

"Connect, don't control."
Ghislaine Caulat

Those who think it's enough to attack the question directly, right at the start of the meeting, have missed an important point: we are all social beings. The need to feel trust, make personal connection and be seen doesn't diminish just because you're sitting at opposite ends of the phone or the video link. Actually, it's probably the other way around: the need can grow*.

Put time into relationship building
at the start of your virtual meetings

We aren't all exactly the same on the need-to-be-seen. About 30% of us prefer either facts or results over relationship, while about 70% prefer relationships over facts and results.

It's naïve to think you have full control over the participants' thoughts, feelings and behaviour, especially in a virtual meeting where you might not even see what the other person is doing. So you should work to create trust and good cooperation. With the same goals and vision your participants will want to reach what you want.

Antoni Lacinai:

> *"I recall a few years back when I had a number of sessions' coaching with a manager in western Sweden. In professional coaching the client needs to greatly trust the coach since they share sensitive information and also personal feelings. The interesting thing is that this manager was the first one I coached without once meeting him in person. So it is possible to develop trust virtually, it just requires more effort."*

This is why you should build some time into your planning to cultivate relationships in your virtual meetings. If the group isn't too big you can let everyone say something – just a Hello, or something about the weather, or the view from the office window, or the food in the company canteen – at the start of the meeting. It doesn't have to take a long time but it shows that you care.

That said, we firmly believe that 100% want to feel certain trust in their co-workers and the meeting leader, and that it's harder to establish a deeper relation in a virtual meeting than in a physical, though it's far from impossible. Groups with more trust also perform better.

Maintain full focus in the virtual meeting

Raise your hand if you have ever misunderstood someone, or if someone has misinterpreted you. This problem exists in good old-fashioned physical gatherings but in virtual meetings it's way more severe.

> *Everything is magnified virtually*

An email that you send in haste might hurt the recipient or make them angry even though you didn't mean to do so. You just wanted to be quick and make yourself clear.

If you are interrupted while you speak in a phone meeting it probably annoys you more than in a physical meeting since you can't see that person – read the body language or the eye-signal that they want to say something – and so you get caught off-guard.

Then, what can you do? Here are three tips!

- **Don't interrupt.** Let whoever is speaking finish. Use the tools at your disposal in your virtual meeting system. Many have a sort of "raise-your-hand" function or a chat window. It could be a good alternative to something verbal that might rock the boat.
- **Be quiet.** The best way to listen is to be interested and to stay quiet. Of course, to be quiet means to not speak out loud, but you should learn

to still your inner voice – the frustrated interrupter that is spoiling your focus on the wisdom coming down the line.

- **Use the MUTE function.** During phone meetings we have heard rustling of candy paper, toilets being flushed, the meowing of cats, sausage being fried, chewing mouths... and of course comments that weren't meant for the group to hear. Please mute yourself!

To multitask or not to multitask? That is the question...

We admit: we were very surprised when experts were not in agreement on this one!

One camp says it's wrong to do other things while you are part of a meeting. The same way it's hard to keep up with what is being said in a physical meeting if you are on Facebook, reading mails or texting, it's as hard, or maybe even harder, to keep up in virtual meetings. Typical advice:

- **No conversations on the side.** Remember that your other conversations are heard or noticed whether you are in a video meeting or a phone meeting. Muting yourself won't help when you are on camera. Besides, you lose track of the topic.
- **Observe/listen to the one who is speaking.** On video it clearly shows if you are focusing on anything other than the meeting.
- **Be mentally present.** You only are if you are focusing on the meeting only.

Then there is the other camp that disagrees. The same way you can't tell if a person in a physical meeting is actually listening or thinking about something else, you can't be sure – or expect – that participants in a virtual meeting are fully present all the time. Typical advice:

- **Take responsibility for yourself.** We are all adults and you know best what is best for you and how your time is best spent.
- **Be more productive.** If the meeting is about something you aren't interested in, do something else as well.
- **Hear what is spoken.** Even if you aren't listening closely you should still be there for when a topic comes up that you can contribute to.

Despite all this, our conclusion is clear:

You can't do two complicated things at once

By complicated things we mean activities like writing a demanding mail – one where you work hard for clarity and good manners – while at the same time trying to follow a discussion on a quite different topic.

If you try to follow two people talking at the same time, your memory of either's speech will likely be zero.

If the meeting has one point you contribute to and the rest is a waste of time, it's better if you ask to be contacted when it's your turn. Either that, or warn the meeting leader that you won't be taking an active part, but rather listening passively to maybe pick up some useful information. If the meeting leader agrees to that, you can mute yourself and hope that your radar senses when something more is needed.

Another alternative is that the entire meeting be redesigned so that every participant who feels that way is always online, always contribuvting. If you are leader of a meeting like that, this may require more energy – more cracking of the whip – from you, but that's life. We come down on this side:

Don't multitask. Don't permit multitasking.

What are we doing during a phone meeting?

The company Intercall made a survey, a year or so ago, where they examined what people did during a phone meeting. 82% admitted to doing other things during the conversation, including:

- 63% send mails and 44% send texts
- 55% cook or eat
- 47% go to the bathroom
- 43% use social media
- 25% play videogames
- 21% shop online

Everyone who thinks these meetings are effective: raise your hand...
Source: The magazine *Telecom today*

Be on time... right on time!

Realise that all technical solutions come with guaranteed ('possible') problems. As Murphy's Law (loosely translated) puts it:

If technology can fail, it will fail.

In a physical meeting you can be pretty sure that the conference room has been double-booked, or the whiteboard pens have run out of juice, or the paper used for notes has run out, or the projector is incompatible with your laptop.

In a virtual meeting the technology will most likely not bend to your will. It's almost a law of nature. We have seen the most experienced techies forced to fall back from video to phone in a meeting. We have experienced first-hand how our computer broke down half an hour before a webinar, causing us to eventually be late to our own meeting. We have ourselves hosted webinars where we thought everything was working perfectly... until we saw the recording of fuzzy-crackly video. We have experienced lots of phone meetings where participants have been cut off and then had problems reconnecting.

Surely, you have too. So do check what you can – in advance.

Have the participants be on time as well. As a meeting leader you should be finished with setting up your tech and testing it 10-15 minutes before the meeting starts, and have a plan B ready just in case friend Murphy lends a hand.

The meeting leader should ideally be ahead of time. For a meeting starting at, say, 11.10 you can start the Hellos at 11.00 sharp. That gives you, and them, ten minutes to grapple with any technical issues.

(Ten minutes is just an example by the way. Five could be enough, or you might need twenty. It depends on how stable the equipment and connectivity are, as well as how experienced your participants are with the technology at hand.)

Keep time zones in mind

If you have a global organisation, on top of this you need to think about when you'll hold your meeting. Just because it's comfortable for you to have it at 14.00 Central European Time doesn't mean it's nice for the people at 5.00 am in San Francisco and 21.00 in Kuala Lumpur. You won't be very popular if you hold your meetings at inconvenient times for your participants. Maybe – as a considerate and democratic leader – you should be the one to suffer.

Sit in different locations

A tip we've acquired during our research, though never experienced ourselves, is that all participants should be in different locations during virtual meetings.

If some participants are in the same friendly room while others are alone somewhere else, it can make the loners feel isolated and shut out, while the happy gang make small talk in whispers and pass notes across the table. Not a level playing field. Level it – separate rooms, everybody!

We know it's rare, but there are organisations with virtual teams that do work this way, perhaps because the home team are scattered along corridors or between floors anyway

Don't have any disturbances around you

A common blunder is to be on the move while at the same time sitting around the virtual meeting table. On a train, in the car, at a festival, lining up at airport departures, behind the church at your sister's wedding, over the stove fixing the kids' TV snack... multitasking across the work-life balance. Not good.

OK, OK. Sometimes it's unavoidable. If you have a long daily commute, virtual communication on a train (from a quiet corner, please) is better than no communication.

Learn the technology well

There are no shortcuts, no corner-cutting. Beware wishful thinking! As meeting leader, you should know the technological platforms better than any of the participants.

To use the technology to its full potential – hosting a webinar, for example – when you want participants free to chat, you have to know what you're doing. We have mentioned buttons for voting and quiz functions. We have also seen virtual breakout rooms, where the group can be divided into buzz-groups in small virtual rooms, then called back to plenary to share what they've achieved. Find out what features that your tools offer and use the ones that fit your meeting.

But you can't plan such smart methods if you don't know how to run them. Once you know what works, you have to train yourself to manage the system – and that includes the (inevitable?) troubleshooting.

Phone meeting services often have support that can be called when in need, so learn the phone's shortcut/speed dial to get help quickly (eg # 0).

It's possible that you are already one of the few who stay on top of technology developments and act as your own IT support. If so, congratulations! If not:

> *Learn the technology well*

Get good stuff – for everyone
Give everyone the right conditions to be able to perform their best. The right software, the right hardware, the right bandwidth. It's hard to have a good conversation if a cheap and nasty microphone is making noises. It's hard to have a good video meeting over shaky broadband. If the technology doesn't allow you to show slides online you should send them, labelled, in advance and have a phone meeting instead.

Make game rules including the use of technology
In addition to the set of rules for physical meetings, we suggest you also make a list for virtual meetings. We have voiced our opinions on several points but that doesn't mean you agree. The answers to the following questions are a good base:

- What technology should you use for different meetings and scenarios?
- What to do if the technology malfunctions? Who does what to fix it?
- Who is responsible for checking the technology to begin with?
- What changes when new and improved technology becomes available?
- Do you dive straight into the point at hand right when the meeting starts, or should you talk about something else first?
- When are the meetings held, during worktime or whenever?
- Do we have clear, formalised titles on our mails and meeting invitations or are we allowed to be as creative as we like?
- How do we know who does what after the meeting? Action points, notes and so on?
- Who is responsible for the competence plan that makes sure all meeting leaders have the same skills?

Don't get too attached to one technology
It's easy to get comfortable with a technical platform. It's quite common.

The more time you spend mastering technology Type X, the less inclined you are to switch to Type Y. Just look at how few migrate between Apple and Google phones.

Remember that some technical solutions are better for some situations and others for others. Think about what you need and then decide what method suits those needs.

> *"To a man with a hammer,*
> *everything looks like a nail"*
> Mark Twain

Keep track of who is speaking – and who isn't

In a physical meeting it's easy to know who's speaking. Just use your eyes. In a virtual meeting it's much harder. There are two obstacles:

1. You aren't sure who has the word or who butting in as if he (it's usually a "he" that interrupts) has the word.
2. It's harder to know who isn't speaking.

There are ways to handle this. We will get to that under tips for different meeting methods. For now, we'll just say:

1. The person speaking starts with his or her name, then 'labels' their contribution. This is also good for summarising "action points" after the meeting: each person gives his/her name and states what they are going to do.
2. Keep an eye (or ear) out for anyone being quiet constantly. Activate them if you feel like you want to get them going.

> *"I notice you're quiet and I wonder..."*

Don't be afraid of silence. It's not necessarily the same thing as being absent; some people have a more reserved style. Maybe they are more introverted; maybe they don't want to take up as much space as some others do; maybe it's a cultural thing. Take the silence on board and say something like *"I notice you're quiet and I wonder..."*

Volume tip: If there's more than one person speaking in a meeting, set the volume to equal for everyone. It's tough to listen to 'shouts' mixed with 'whispers' and 'mumbles'.

Keep it short

Being alert during meetings is tiring, and the longer a meeting lasts, the tougher it gets. Being alert during plainly bad physical meetings, filled with densely-packed slides and the constant churning of voices, is almost impossible, and it's definitely not easier in a virtual meeting. There, it's generally even more difficult to maintain focus. You're sitting by yourself, you can't get anything from the body language of the others, audio quality can be low, the video poor and so on. This requires greater concentration and it's very tiring. Make it easy on yourself:

> *Keep virtual meetings shorter*
> *than corresponding physical ones*

Our clients have told us about virtual meetings that last hours and hours. They say it drains their energy, and doubt whether it really is beneficial to have such meetings. It's not!

The usual recommendation is that a virtual meeting should last a maximum of two hours. We think that's far too long. Shorter meetings are better, more fun and more effective.

If you still want long meetings: throw some breaks in there for people to recover a bit. Use methods to create involvement.

Twenty years ago it was said by communication coaches that an audience can maintain focus for 20 minutes before something has to happen. Today, that number is said to be 3-4 minutes. Variation is key.

Utilise asynchronous communication

We know, we've already talked about this. We'll do it again. Just a bit.

Far too many meetings have a single goal: to extract information. It's an ineffective way to meet. The participants will only remember a fraction of what was said, while they remember most of what they themselves chipped in.

In virtual meetings it's even harder. To just sit there and passively listen doesn't get you engaged in the topic, nor does it help you remember.

Make information available offline (before the meeting) and the time you have for the meeting can be used to convert the information to knowledge that the participants can remember and use.

Inform prior. Discuss during.

Some information you might not want to release prior to the meeting. There are numerous reasons for this that we won't get into here. We ask you to think about how much you want the participants to *remember* afterwards, what they will *feel* and finally what they will *do*. If you want them to remember much you will need to involve them in some way. Learning-by-doing.

3.
Meeting tips
for different types
of technology

Meeting tips for different types of virtual technology

Now we'll get to the more specific recommendations for each configuration of virtual meeting, such as phone calls, video, web, email etc.

Some of the previous tips will be repeated here. Others are new and specific. Some tips suit more than one platform, and if so we have put them in more than one list.

We have also provided a blank page after each segment for you to write your own personal tips and experiences. Maybe you could let us know your jottings some time, so we can spread the word? We'd appreciate that!

Tips for the phone meeting

- **Sit by yourself.** Everybody should be connected the same way. A mix of some people sitting together and others by themselves makes for a worse meeting.
- **Be somewhere quiet.** Don't sit at your desk where there are hundreds of things to distract you. Don't be at the train station, in the coffee lounge, the supermarket. Constructive listening is hard enough...
- **Use headsets that cover both ears.** Good quality ones, too. It makes it that much easier to hear what people are saying and it makes it easier to focus.

- **Make sure you have enough battery life left.** If you're using a cellphone or a wireless phone of some kind you need enough juice to last the whole meeting and preferably more, just to be safe.
- **Be on time.** Good time. As a meeting leader it's good if you are the first one in the phone conference. A meeting leader should be ready five minutes before the actual meeting starts, just to make sure the technology is working and to greet everyone.
- **Don't speak too loudly among people.** It's not at all necessary for everyone around you to hear what you're talking about. They probably don't want to and shouldn't hear it. Though it's preferable if you aren't around people at all.
- **Speak clearly.** Any small amount of noise will make it difficult to understand. Articulate, emphasize and pause to make your message as understandable as possible.
- **Make room for breaks.** If the meeting is of the longer kind, or if there will be natural changes of topic, you can have a smaller or longer break.
- **Eat and do your business before the meeting.** You can't focus as well when you are hungry, thirsty, tired. Research has shown that judges tend to give harsher sentences before lunch than they do just after breakfast.
- **Be mentally present.** How else could you possibly contribute to the meeting?
- **Slow down.** In a phone meeting you can gain by reducing the tempo of the conversation to better understand.
- **Listen carefully.** You can notice a lot more just by listening. Through both accentuation and silence you can catch, for example, emotions and the speakers' opinion.
- **Write down the participants.** That way it's easier to know who is talking at all times.
- **Mute yourself when not speaking.** Turn off your input sound to lower the noise in the call. It helps everyone.
- **Don't fiddle with things that make noise.** Even though it might not be very loud, it will still be heard. Keyring? Hole-punch? Coffee spoon and saucer?

- **Don't chew.** Eating while in a meeting? It sets a bad example!
- **Tell everyone you're speaking.** Say your name before you start talking and nobody will be confused. This is especially important when there are more than three people in your meeting.
- **Try not to interrupt anyone.** In a phone meeting it can be hard but it's possible. If you must… if you do… apologize.
- **Take notes.** Either yourself or through someone else you appoint. You don't have to write down everything that is said but it's good to at least get the decisions and tasks allocated on paper.
- **Every person that receives a task, repeats the task and the time given for it.** This is best done at the end of the meeting so that nothing vital is missed – no nasty repercussions.
- **Have good ways to start and finish.** As a meeting leader you can create good conditions by getting everyone going at the start of a meeting and then finishing off nicely without stress. Build relationships, summarise and agree on who does what next.

Own notes

Tips for the video meeting

- **Sit by yourself.** Everybody should be connected the same way. A mix of some people sitting together and others by themselves makes for a worse meeting.
- **Prepare carefully.** Technology will sometimes just not work. Far too many video meetings end with the group giving up and switching to a phone meeting. It's boring and it drains your energy. Testing everything with good time left before the meeting starts will give you time to solve any problems that you might come across.
- **Get closer.** Don't sit too far from the camera; get closer (or zoom in). It makes for a better atmosphere and feeling.
- **Make room for breaks.** If the meeting is of the longer kind, or if there naturally will be interruptions to change topic, you can have a smaller or longer break.
- **Eat and do your business before the meeting.** You can't focus as well when you are hungry, thirsty, tired. Research has shown that judges tend to give harsher sentences before lunch than they do after breakfast.
- **Be mentally present.** How else could you possibly contribute to the meeting?
- **Look at the camera when speaking.** Don't look at your monitor. Precious eye contact is easy to lose compared to physical meetings. Less comfort, less trust, less creativity which makes it less comfortable.
- **Mute yourself when not speaking.** Turn off your input sound to lower the noise in the call. It helps everyone.
- **Find ways to involve.** Chat, voting, discussions, questions for randomly chosen people are a few ways.
- **Mix it up.** Instead of just looking at each other's' faces you could maybe add a video or some pictures (relevant of course). This will break the monotony and make the participants more alert again.
- **Record the meeting.** One advantage is that you can often record the video meeting so you can watch it later if there is something you need to check, and anyone not able to participate can watch the meeting afterwards.

Own notes

Tips for the web meeting (webinar)

In a webinar there is usually one speaker and the rest are listeners. It's comparable to a virtual theatre. In a web broadcast there can be audience in the same physical room as well as audience listening and watching through the Internet.

- **Be on time to go over the technology.** The more technology the bigger the risk of something bad happening. Make sure everything works on your end.
- **Get closer.** Don't sit too far from the camera; get closer (or zoom in). It makes for a better atmosphere and feeling.
- **Show slides if you have to.** Sometimes it's harder to follow the presentation if the speaker is using slides that are not shown to the virtual audience.
- **Avoid long presentations.** If it lasts more than 5-10 minutes it can get tough to focus.
- **Let the chat be free.** Give the participants the chance to reflect and ask questions in the chat function that is usually available.
- **Stop and interact with the audience.** After each subject, after each big message, you should stop for a moment and answer questions as well as going through the chat to see if anything noteworthy has happened or been asked there. This will generate more energy and enthusiasm. It's not a bad idea to do this with "process slides" that don't have any information but rather some text like: Questions?
- **Pause.** If the meeting is of the longer variety or if there are natural pauses in the meeting when changing subject, you can have a minor (or major) break to help people recover slightly.
- **Look at the camera when speaking.** Don't look at your monitor. Precious eye contact specifically is something that's easy to lose compared to physical meetings which makes it less comfortable.
- **Use the shared "spaces"** if you want people to create text or illustrations on a e.g. a virtual whiteboard.

- **Record the meeting.** One advantage is that you can often record the video meeting so you can watch it later if there is something you need to check, and anyone not able to participate can watch the meeting afterwards.

Own notes

Tips for email

Think about the structure and layout of the mail

- **A maximum of three rows per paragraph** is a good guideline. Our brain has a harder time reading off a monitor than a piece of paper.

- **Avoid capitals**, as they are tougher to read and can be perceived as YELLING – perhaps causing unwanted reactions.

- **Read through your mail before you send it** to avoid misspelling, to make a check on the structure of the text, and to see if it carries just the right message. If the purpose of sending an email is to have the receiver(s) understand something, it's important to read the mail from their perspective, as best you can.

- **Only keep your email up when working on a mail.** When working in real time it's often distracting to constantly get notified (Ping!) when an email comes in. Therefore we recommend you close the program/page when not working with anything mail-related.

- **Relax.** When we are stressed out or annoyed we tend to both read and write emails irrationally.

We're switching gears here and we'll give you some questions to think about:

- **How should the headline look?** Should you add tags such as FYI (for your information) or FYA (for your action)? Should you use longer or shorter headlines?

- **How long should the mail be?** Shorter ones where you don't even have to scroll to read the full message? What about attached files?

- **Who should receive this mail?** Just the one it's for? Should others get a copy as well? In that case, how should you use CC or BCC, not to clutter the inboxes of those who don't need to know?

- **What kind of content is OK to send by email?** Is it OK to send private emails? Are confidential mails OK? Is it OK to resolve conflicts through email? How should you handle it if the answer is No? Is it OK to email an answer to mail that you perceive as negative? Should you instead call this person? Is it OK to use mail to confirm what you have agreed upon?

- **When should a mail be answered?** Immediately? Within a day or two? A week? Does this need to be written in the headline of the mail? How often should you check your inbox? Two times a day? Keep it up all day? Is it OK to not answer? Or wait till you receive a reminder?

Own notes

Questions regarding voicemail and SMS

- **When should you leave messages?** When shouldn't you? What kind of message are you using, for example when you are unreachable for some reason? Is it OK to leave a message stating it's not possible to leave a message?
- **How long should spoken messages be/how long should an SMS be?** How much detail should you go into? What is the optimal time/text length for you?
- **When should you reply (if needed)?** Immediately? Within a day or two? A week? Does this need to be written in the headline of the mail? How often should you check your inbox? Twice a day? Keep it up all day? Is it OK to not answer? Or wait till you receive a reminder?

Own notes

Adapted methods for virtual meetings

Sometimes it requires something extra to get the creativity going, or reach a decision in a clear way when communicating virtually. We have chosen three methods:

Brainwriting

Instead of *brainstorming* with everyone gathered in a room pumping out as many ideas as possible, you can choose to work with *brainwriting*, which can work something like this:

- Split into **groups** of 3-5. This can be handled through mail.
- Each **person** writes **three solutions** to the problem you want new ideas for, in a **mail** and sends it to one of the members of the group (in a set rotation).
- **The receiver** looks at the three ideas and **produces three more** based on these associations, new thoughts and so on. These are then sent to the next person according to the rotation.
- Once it's gone full circle you will get your original ideas back but now with the rest of the group's ideas added on.
- All these **ideas** can be **handed out** for **reflection** or **feedback** or **voting**.
- In the virtual meeting you will then have a **top list** that you can work on.

The decision meeting

There are four ways for a group to make a decision:

- **Democratic** decisions, the majority winning
- **Autocratic** decisions, the boss deciding
- **Unanimous**, everyone agreeing to one thing
- **Consensus**, not everyone necessarily agreeing, but all buying in and executing what has been decided

Research shows that consensus decisions are actually the best (according to the book *Managers guide to virtual teams*, by Fisher & Fisher). Interesting indeed! The Swedish consensus way of working might not be so bad after all.

The process might look something like this:

- Define **the problem**.
- **Decide** how you should act if you **can't reach a consensus** decision.
- **Plan some time** (asynchronous/offline) to reflect and think.
- Everyone **shares** their **thoughts** offline or online.
- Look for **similarities** in your thoughts. Look for differences. Explain and clarify your points.
- Let **everyone** speak their opinion.

Before you summaries and decide you can make sure everyone is OK with the way forward.

In a video meeting you can let everyone give:

- **Thumbs up** if they support the suggestion.
- **Thumbs sideways** if they support it, with reservation.
- **Thumbs down** if they don't support the suggestion in its current state.

If you get all thumbs up or some sideways you can move on and decide. If there are some thumbs down: discuss some more. If you can't reach a decision you go to plan B, which means choosing a decision model acceptable to all... or anyway most.

For phone meetings you can do the same thing but in this case you should swap the thumb signals for "traffic lights":

- **"Green light"**: supporting the suggestion
- **"Yellow light"**: supporting it, with reservation
- **"Red light"**: not supporting the suggestion in its current state

If you get all green lights or just a few yellow ones you can make a decision. The process is the same as the video meeting show of thumbs.

Shared goal/purpose/vision etc

If you work with shared workspaces online at the same time as having, for example, a phone meeting or similar, you can perform this exercise to reach a common purpose:

- Everyone **mails** brief suggestions – 3-5 words.
- **Gather** all the sentences in the virtual **workspace** (writing space).
- Look for **similarities** and group them up.
- Look for **differences** and discuss.
- **Form a sentence** that you can all stand behind.

Our final thoughts

Maybe you're reading this book virtually – as a pdf in on your computer, tablet or smartphone or e-pub on an eReader. Maybe you're reading it in paper format. We bring this up to make the point that all variants have their place and that different preferences and needs control the way we communicate.

When we started diving into the constantly flowing, turbid waters surrounding virtual meetings we had some preconceptions:
- A good meeting in the physical world is almost always better than a good virtual meeting.
- A bad meeting in the physical world is almost always better than a bad virtual meeting.
- If you are a skilled meeting leader in physical meetings, you still need to be even better when hosting virtual meetings.
- If you are a bad meeting leader in physical meetings it will make for an even worse virtual meeting.

Our research has led us to nuance that picture a bit.
- Some meetings would never even happen if not for virtual meetings. What would we lose if that was the case?
- Sometimes good enough is best. That can be the case with virtual meetings.
- You can have good virtual meetings.

- As a meeting leader you DO need to prepare more and be a bit more skilled as a leader when having virtual meetings. You also need to understand how to use the technology to its fullest potential or else you will lose out on a lot.
- You can save time, money and the environment with virtual meetings.

One of the real experts in virtual leadership is Ghislaine Caulat. Her words (loosely translated) are:

> *"If we use our normal way of thinking, saying and acting, in the virtual world, the results won't be any good. If we instead focus on doing better, we can reach great success."*

If you feel like we missed any pros and cons: **Tell us.**
If you feel like we missed any practical tips and tricks: **Tell us.**
If you feel like we did well with this guide: **Tell us.**

Once we've collected enough new tips and thoughts from you, we will make a guide 2.0 where you are quoted.

Good luck with your virtual meetings!

A special thank-you

Many have participated and we want to give special thanks to these four people:
- Ghislaine Caulat, expert in virtual communication and virtual leadership
- Bengt Littorin from Naturvårdsverket (Environmental Protection Agency), expert of many years in "travel-free meetings"
- Pär Stenstierna, founder of Videokonferensbolaget
- Charlotte Wahlin, head of staff at Volvo Cars and the one who got us to actually write the book

You have helped us through the embryo stage of the book with your wisdom and without you the book would either be a lot worse or just not exist. Thank you!

And thank you who read this book! Best of luck with your virtual meetings.

Antoni Lacinai & Mike Darmell

More books by us

Antoni Lacinai & Mike Darmell
Make Meetings Work. 2015 e-book (Bookboon.com and Amazon.com)
Make Meetings Work. 2016 Paperback (Amazon.com)

Antoni Lacinai:
Understanding Body Language. 2016 (Amazon.com)

Other books have been written by the authors but they are, to date, in Swedish.

Lightning Source UK Ltd.
Milton Keynes UK
UKHW020636140122
397142UK00009B/623